BUNKER HILL

Last of the Lofty Mansions

Looking like a combination of several exotic movie sets, the garish facade of the Angel's Flight upper station gave the unprepared passenger little warning of the steep ride in store for him once he pushed open the ornate door on the right. The passenger leaving with eyes cast down must have been little impressed. Or perhaps he had experienced the ride so many times the thrill was gone forever.

BUNKER HILL

Last of the Lofty Mansions

Text: WILLIAM PUGSLEY

Photography and

Photographic Research: ROY W. HANKEY

Trans-Anglo Books

Corona del Mar, California

Library of Congress Cataloging in Publication Data

Pugsley, William.
   Bunker Hill, last of the lofty mansions.

   1. Bunker Hill, Los Angeles. 2. Los Angeles--
History. I. Hankey, Roy W. II. Title.
F869.L86B866   979.4'94'04   77-76013
ISBN 0-07046-046-3

BUNKER HILL:
Last of the Lofty Mansions

By WILLIAM PUGSLEY

Photography: Roy W. Hankey

Copyright © MCMLXXVII by Roy W. Hankey and William Pugsley

FIRST EDITION

Library of Congress Catalog Card Number: 77-076013

ISBN: 0-87046-046-3

BOOK DESIGN: HANK JOHNSTON

•

Printed and Bound in the United States of America

Editorial Director: Spencer Crump

Published by Trans-Anglo Books,
P.O. Box 38, Corona del Mar, California 92625

INTRODUCTION

·

There was a time when ladies and gentlemen living in three-story turreted mansions entertained the wealthy, famous, and titled on top of a hill in the middle of a city called Los Angeles. Custom-built carriages would line up for blocks to discharge their socially elite passengers.

Those who lived in other parts of the city and were able to gaze up at these fanciful happenings did so with unabashed awe. Colored lights and other rainbow illuminations moved across the horizon of this magical hill, giving more factual evidence of the wonder that was forever floating above.

This was the era of McKinley and Teddy Roosevelt, the acquisition of the Philippine Islands, and the forming of trade unions across the nation. People of America were learning how to live well and display their wealth in an ostentatious manner. Those with money who moved to southern California soon became aware of the advantages of an area to be called Bunker Hill. This lofty elevation offered the new residents a certain social and moral aloofness over the surrounding population. They became lords and ladies in wooden clapboard castles. Servants would either climb the hundreds of steps on the side of the hill or ride an incredible cable railway called Angel's Flight.

All of that glitter and hushed elegance is gone now forever. Not even remnants of the reinforced concrete foundations can be found in the empty fields. Still it is possible to live again in those halcyon times if only by imagination.

In the following pages you will be taken up to the very crest of this fabled promontory and personally introduced to many of the distinguished members of that majestic inner circle. Some of them have left behind valuable legacies to mankind; others have been satisfied to merely fade away into obscurity.

The hill itself should also be considered just as much of a vital personality as those who lived on top of it — for without its continual aura of grandeur, none of this fabulous pageantry could ever have taken place.

– – –

The author expresses his appreciation to the individuals and organizations who assisted in preparing this book.

A special and heart-felt thanks goes to our good friend, Gerald Dixon, whose faith and encouragement helped make this book possible.

We extend our appreciation for the use of photographs to Security Pacific National Bank, Title Insurance and Trust Company, the Los Angeles City Department of Water and Power, Bekins Moving and Storage Company, Los Angeles Museum of Science and Industry, the Los Angeles *Herald-Examiner*, the Sunkist Growers Association, and the Los Angeles Public Library (with special thanks to Mr. Tom Owens).

ROY W. HANKEY
WILLIAM PUGSLEY

Los Angeles, California

Viewing the current landscape of Bunker Hill from the top floor of the nearby courthouse on First Street, the giant office buildings on the horizon appear as menacing chess pieces about to checkmate any unsuspecting trespasser who would dare threaten their continued existence. The rows of cars down below seem like harmless toys, yet these machines are the prime smog-makers of the city.

BUNKER HILL

Last of the Lofty Mansions

Perched atop the sloping hills at the eastern edge of the present-day central Los Angeles business district, you could see for miles on the clear, smogless days of the early 1900s.

To the right were the towering San Gabriel Mountains, sloping down to the trail through Cahuenga Pass and the Hollywood Hills. To the southwest were the Santa Monica Mountains and the Pacific Ocean.

Dominating the central Los Angeles area was one of Southern California's wealthiest and most picturesque areas: Bunker Hill, with its lofty, Victorian-style mansions.

The day was December 31, 1901, and the wealthy residents of Bunker Hill gathered with the curious from other areas for a momentous event: the opening of the Angel's Flight Railway, carrying passengers from Third and Hill Streets up the steep grade to Bunker Hill.

Two cars ran at the same time up the 33 per cent grade over 335 feet. Each balanced the other so that a minimum of power was required. If you preferred not to pay the one-cent fare, you could climb the 207 steps adjoining the rails. The builder of Angel's Flight was Colonel J. W. Eddy, 69 years old when the railway opened and an individual whose career included experience as a lawyer and engineer.

Atop Bunker Hill where the railway terminated was an observation tower presenting a spectacular view of the surrounding plains, virtually uninhabited during the early 1900s.

While Bunker Hill already was noted for its mansions, the Angel's Flight Railway spurred its development and made the area more accessible for those who wished to gaze at the ornate houses.

Residents of the exclusive Bunker Hill neighborhood traveled up and down these 100 yards almost every hour of the day and night, giving little thought to the intricate equipment surrounding them at that moment.

The twelve-inch solid iron wheels were bolted directly to the hardwood frame and the cars ran on a thirty-inch gauge track made of 40-pound iron. There was no steel frame running underneath the body but the little coaches were absolutely safe.

The weather made little difference to the solitary operator who was sequestered in a rectangular cabin at the top of the hill. Ten years from this date an electrically operated turnstyle would be installed to prevent late passengers from boarding the moving vehicles. This would further insure an accident-free journey.

This was a time of honor and glory for an area between Temple and Sixth Streets in Los Angeles, California, called Bunker Hill as a tribute to the first large-scale engagement of the American Revolution.

Influential businessmen would soon construct

7

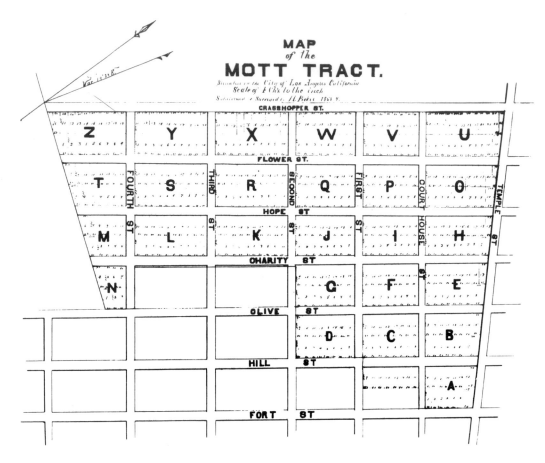

MAP
of the
MOTT TRACT.

The old Mott Tract, scaled in 1868, was later called Bunker Hill. Some of the streets have been changed through the years: Grasshopper to Figueroa and Charity Street to Grand. Of course the original plots no longer exist; vacant lots or double-decked parking facilities have taken their place.

castle-like mansions on the lofty crests of this majestic rise. No one at this period of the century would have ever guessed that one day all of this prominence would disappear without a trace.

There was too much material grandeur to observe in all directions. It was like gazing at the stars and knowing in your heart that they would be there forever because that was the way of the world. Much was to happen, however, between those sublime years of the late nineteenth century and the coming era of so-called progressive city planning.

For the moment, the men and women with imagination and social consciousness gathered in this one district of Los Angeles and in a special way hovered over the city as though they were the high priests of elegance. Land was comparatively cheap in these days when you consider that in 1870 twenty acres bounded by Second, Fourth, Hill, and Charity Streets sold for the remarkable sum of $517.00. This is the equivalent of buying a new car today for about five dollars and some loose change!

One of the first homes on the Hill was built by a man who literally saw stars. Max Heindel was a well-known writer of books on astronomy. The elevation which he gave his private residence was

certainly not enough to allow him a clearer view of the heavens but symbolically he was in a most august region where his inner self was assured of a peace not really possible on the flat land down below.

Originally the house was painted by a Spanish contractor who prided himself on his work. Many coats were applied and in the hot, concentrated Los Angeles sun they dried quickly.

It is not known if Mr. Heindel was given a guarantee as to the longevity of the paint but the wooden clap boards were never painted again and yet the hint of the original color still remained many decades later.

According to several city records, the Heindel mansion was one of the last residences to be torn down. In all those tumultuous years no one in particular was defending its existence; still it seemed to be able to sustain itself against change regardless of the environmental pressures surrounding it at all times.

Lady McDonald from Canada visited Los Angeles in the early 1900s and was immediately taken by the quaint isolation of the Hill. She surprised her friends and relatives back home by deciding to build a home on one of the narrow streets. Perhaps she knew instinctively that she

In 1860 Los Angeles could claim only one bona fide reservoir, located in the Plaza and holding only about 80,000 gallons. Balanced on top of a brick foundation, the metal tank was held together by bolts and tie-rods.

Imagining this much open space in the Los Angeles area is difficult, even if the year is 1885. This view is west on Third Street from Grand Avenue. High on the Hill is the Belmont Hotel.

The artful advertising methods of Madison Avenue were
not yet to be exposed to the builders and planners of Los
Angeles in the early 1900s. J. W. Eddy had a flair of his own
that was extremely effective for his time. The Colonel personally designed the Angel's Flight brochure, and it was
circulated daily to visitors at the various nearby hotels.
Notice the telephone numbers listed for information. Only
four digits were necessary. Not everyone could afford the
luxury of such a service, and the phone companies were a
long way off from automatic dialing.

could expand on her active social life by establishing her residence in the warmer climate of southern California.

Los Angeles social life received a definite uplift when this enterprising lady came upon the scene. Her catered parties were memorable events since many international personages were often on hand.

She was the first in Los Angeles to install a hydraulic elevator in her home. Guests would sometimes line up to "take a ride" to the top floor and down again. The Lady herself would often be at the controls and in her elegant manner take off into the spaces above as though she were a future female astronaut on her merry way to a planetary landing.

Next door to the McDonald estate was the antithesis of the social elite. Not that D. F. Donigan wasn't a respectable man, but you might say that he was self-made with strong individualistic opinions. He knew the meaning of hard work and liked to kick his shoes off after a hard day with his own contracting business.

His 20-room mansion in the 300 block on Bunker Hill was a mixture of classic style and period ostentatiousness. The brightly painted gingerbread porte-cochere and the elongated carriage house in the rear gave Mr. Donigan's mansion that distinctive mark of opulence he so dearly desired.

Whether he was socially on the level with Lady McDonald made little difference. He was able to offer an imaginative talent to the continuing growth of Los Angeles. His contracting company built the first railroad from Los Angeles to Pasadena; it is now a part of the Santa Fe. His farsighted knowledge as an engineer made him an indispensable advisor. His suggestion that the Broadway tunnel be brought up to a certain level saved thousands of dollars in future construction.

Probably it was his idiosyncrasies which finally set him apart from the other residents on the Hill. For investment purposes he purchased a ranch at the southern extremity of the city. Within two weeks he discovered that it was infested with rats. Being an inventive man, he immediately let it be known to the local children that he would purchase any cat they brought to him for twenty-five cents. Soon the cat population on the Hill took a dangerous plunge down. There was only one person to blame for this catastrophe and Donigan took the brunt of all the complaints in his usual casual manner.

Ironically, the wife of Max Heindel, a renowned astronomer of his time, was intensely interested in astrology. She was the co-founder of the Rosicrucian Fellowship and often gave lectures on the mystical qualities of the stars in her Bunker Hill home.

That a clique would eventually be established amongst the residents of the Hill is not difficult to understand. Living on Bunker Hill was much like residing on a distant island with only a 100-yard cable car attaching them to the "mainland."

The social list of that time included some illustrious names: Dr. John C. Zahn was a man who believed that material wealth should be displayed, not with arrogance but with quiet style and perhaps an occasional flamboyancy.

During the holiday months of November and December, the flickering lights of a lawn party could be observed from this miniature estate. From afar the mixed colored illumination looked like snow volcanos suspended on invisible wires high in the sky.

One of the guests that night might have been the redoubtable Simona Bradbury. As the wife of

The social elite often gathered at the Bradbury mansion at the corner of Hill and Court Streets for parties late into the night. Sometimes carriages were double parked on the narrow street, and in deference, traffic would bypass this intersection until all guests were properly greeted. Although the structure was built to last for centuries, it was razed in 1929.

Colonel Louis W. Bradbury, she commanded a great deal of respect in the quasi-aristocracy of Bunker Hill. The Colonel had made his fortune from a silver mine located in the lower half of California and had decided to make Los Angeles his permanent home.

It was no surprise that he constructed a spacious mansion at Court Street and North Hill after the grand opening of his magnificent office building downtown. Like the ancient pharaohs of Egypt, the Colonel was determined to have his regal crypts which would last long after he had departed from this earth.

Gossip had it that Simona ruled the Bradbury house and probably the Colonel would have agreed. Unfortunately she was unable to control one important event in her own son's life. When John Bradbury married beautiful Lucy Banning everyone considered the union a perfect affiliation. The marriage took place in the Bradbury mansion and the invited guests were dazzled by the crystal chandeliers, Persian rugs, and beveled French mirrors. This event was considered one more sparkling gem in Simona's social crown. By this marriage she was extending her realm of influence and there was no doubt she would use it well.

When the marriage ended in tragedy, Simona went into self-imposed isolation. All the money in the world wasn't able to unite two people who were really unsuitable for one another at the very beginning.

Some of the social events on the Hill were not as maneuvered as the Zahn affairs. A man by the name of Samuel B. Caswell living at the southeast corner of Grand Avenue and Fifth Street had a unique scheme that guaranteed him a full house every Friday night of the week.

Mr. Caswell would call the social reporter on the Los Angeles daily paper and announce that various ladies of the community would entertain at his house the following week. Their lovely daughters would also be in attendance and apparently be unescorted. This was the signal for the blades on the Hill to step forward and see that they were invited also. If Mr. Caswell was a voyeur at heart, then this weekly routine during the summer months must have been very dear to his heart.

People from every conceivable profession came to live on the winding streets of the Hill. A retired clergyman from Chicago by the name of Dr. Edmund Hildreth believed that he could surround he and his family with a tranquility that could

Judge R. M. Widney was a man of direct action and principle. In 1876 he defended a large number of settlers who had disputed titles to lands under the State School Land Act. His speeches and library work on this legal maneuver made a volume of about 800 octavo pages. He refused to enter politics, preferring to work in lines more directly beneficial to his fellow men. This unselfish attitude helped open up Bunker Hill to many families who wanted to make the area their permanent home.

never be threatened. He was a man who often quoted from the bible to make his point. To reaffirm his concept of solidity he hired a local contractor to construct a retaining wall of massive granite blocks that completely encompassed his hilltop house.

The stones were hauled up the side of the crest and there were several harrowing incidents in which the team would have to back up and attempt the heroic push forward one more time.

With all this corporeal protection, the Doctor was still not secure from the daily changes of fortune. On one terrible late Sunday afternoon he was informed that his son had drowned in the wide pool at Silverlake. A few years later his young daughter, Faith, died and this second tragedy almost made a recluse of him.

Tragedy had not finished with this clergyman who had surrounded himself with giant blocks of granite. Dr. George Hunter, a noted scientist who married one of the older Hildreth girls, was

suddenly shot to death by a deranged patient who concealed a revolver beneath the bed sheets.

Life would continue on in the same fashion at the top of the Hill no matter what adversity was happening to one of its members. While others were dying, some still had vibrant plans for the future.

One famous resident of the Hill was Judge R. M. Widney, who helped found the University of Southern California and later became the state's lieutenant governor.

The Judge had a habit of walking home for lunch and he could do this with ease when he lived on the flat land around Spring Street. When his wife got the idea that she wanted to move up with the other socially prominent people on top of Bunker Hill, the journey was not so easy for him.

Something had to be done about that steep walk confronting him every afternoon. The Judge was not one to be stymied by anything as grossly material as a steeply slanting road. His mansion at 310 South Olive had all the conveniences of the time and he had no intention of giving them up during his afternoon recess merely because his legs might give out from under him during an arduous walk home.

A friend was experiencing the same difficulty. E. F. Spence, president of the First National Bank, had left his athletic days far behind. Although he had no intention of walking home for lunch every day, he did feel that some type of accessible transportation was needed from his business to the Bunker Hill area.

Bureaucratic red tape was not as invidious in those early days and a couple of rich influential friends could make things happen if they decided to join forces and get things moving. This was the way that the first horse-drawn street car came into existence and started its run from the Plaza to the base of Bunker Hill.

Few of the passengers might have recognized Judge Widney when he climbed aboard for his quick (three miles an hour) journey home for lunch, but they all had him to thank for this new kind of transportation in the middle of the growing business district of Los Angeles.

It would seem that the Judge somehow attracted various modes of travel to him at all times. In a few years the Angel's Flight was built just a couple of doors south of his mansion. He didn't object to its proximity at all since this completed the link to the Plaza down below.

If the Judge still wanted to walk on a particularly sunny day, he would find an open stairway on the opposite side of the Angel's Flight with 123 healthy steps and ten accommodating ramps. This concrete descent was not constructed for his benefit but rather to insure that the new electric cable railway might never be considered a monopoly. Bunker Hill residents would always have their choice between sitting or standing on their way down the long slanting incline.

Each new arrival to the Hill had their own particular reasons for relocating, but probably that of L. J. Rose was the most poignant. A single calamity eventually forced the Rose family to the west coast.

During one unusually cold winter in the mid-west, one of their young sons developed serious bronchial trouble. From the moment of his first infection his health began to fail. There were no health-giving rays from the sun to cure him and finally on an early clouded morning in November he passed away.

The Rose family mourned for many months and for awhile L. J. Rose became a bitter, cynical man. All of his energies were drained from him and no matter how many times his

understanding neighbors came to his door with good wishes he didn't respond at all.

Fortunately Mr. Rose was a man of many talents and this was to be his ultimate salvation. He had made a fine reputation for himself as a breeder of trotting stock, which opened new vistas in his life.

Finally he was able to reconstruct his thinking, but he knew he could never go back to the same patterns. He had to leave the cold climate of northern Iowa forever and the only sensible direction seemed to be southwest.

Arriving in Los Angeles in the mid-1800s, he immediately investigated the elite Bunker Hill region. The area seemed remote enough and could be a sanctuary against too many inquisitive people.

The breeding of horses was still important to him but now the new climate and atmosphere created another interest. After some preliminary inspections of the local winemakers, L. J. went into business for himself.

Perhaps it was the new environment that was a combination of recluse living and bustling city life or maybe it was just the idea of living up

The residence of Leonard John Rose at the southeast corner of Grand Avenue on Bunker Hill was a palatial showplace of its time. Here is the interior of the sumptuous living room with a crystal chandelier suspended over a black Italian marble table. The rugs were priceless Orientals, and the teak paneling took many months of planning and design before it could be completed.

Deep within the foundation of the Rose mansion at the southeast corner of Fourth and Grand was a unique wine cellar. Rose's 2000-acre vineyard near the San Gabriel Mission supplied all his domestic needs and then some. Fortunately Rose practiced moderation, or tragedy might have struck his family in the years to come.

The light of a new age came to Bunker Hill on New Year's Eve, 1882. Electric arc lights, 150 feet high, were placed at Fourth and Charity (now Grand Avenue) plus seven other nearby locations. At exactly 7:30 p.m. on December 31 the electric lights were turned on, and became illuminated Maypoles that momentarily dazzled the spectators down below. Surely nothing more spectacular than this would ever happen. Man had at last reached the pinnacle of scientific discovery, and there it was for all to view at the very top of beautiful Bunker Hill.

on top of a hill that opened these new intuitive powers. In less than a few years he developed a variety of foreign grapes which are still revered in the winemaking industry.

His wine cellar became the talk of Bunker Hill society and he was never shy about giving a new guest a full tour down the narrow stairway into the dry caverns beneath his palatial home.

Later on in his career he would have to revert back to his old horse breeding talents. When he sustained heavy financial losses through some unfortunate investments, he loaded a car with Stanbeau colts and freighted them into New York when he sold the animals for enough money to recoup his fortune.

It was men and women of L. J. Rose's character who were primarily attracted to Bunker Hill in those early days. These were individuals with wealth and intelligence who wanted to live in comfort and style without giving up completely the challenge of the open spaces — and there were still some left, believe it or not, before the turn of the century.

New neighbors were appearing almost daily now that the Hill had been established as a refuge from the expanding commercialism down below. It was a continual challenge to the architects of the time to build without duplication.

A number of novel styles prevailed during this uninhibited building period; most notably were the state pavilions, Queen Anne, and Eastlake designs.

Eastlake was a hopeful return to simplicity and utilitarianism; Queen Anne might be described as an architectural amalgam that was both showy, fancy, and at extreme times vulgar. Wide rambling verandas, bubbled gables, and small ornate balconies were trademarks of this particular form.

A number of independent builders dismissed so-called tradition. Erratic mansions were built that were arbitrarily decorated with corner towers, spindled verandas and a panorama of colorful stained glass. During a particular brilliant sunset the facade facing the west would become a dazzling splintered glow of tangled prisms and flat surfaces of reflecting glass.

To those who truly wanted to be noticed and remembered by the casual passerbys, diagonal stripes of siding and variegated shingles were necessary added features.

It was generally believed that the wealthy who finally decided to settle within the perimeters of Bunker Hill operated only through legitimate architectural firms. Such was not the case at all! Before even considering a rudimentary foundation, many of these new land owners would thumb through illustrated weeklies for ideas. Whatever struck them as fashionable would then be related to their bewildered builders who could only shrug their shoulders and do the best they could under the circumstances.

Simple hacienda construction was frowned upon. Although this type of architecture had many practical aspects, no one with any kind of social consciousness of the time would have even remotely considered such a plebeian design.

Frame houses became a popular concept

If you had stood on Hill Street in 1886 and looked directly northwest toward Bunker Hill and Third Street you would have been able to wave to the upstairs maid in the Crocker mansion facing you. The small boy leaning against the lamppost in the left hand corner must have been observing the photographer with intense interest. The camera wasn't as popular in those days.

because of the many variations possible. It was chic to be different and there was always a certain mystery as to what function an added room might give to the new owner.

The kitchen and store rooms were usually fastened onto the main square floor plan. Porches could go half way around the house offering deadends to visiting relatives and unwelcome salesmen.

Windows were set into horizontal siding and often framed with multi-colored tiered moldings. And if the owner truly wanted to be considered elegant — and who didn't in those glorious showoff days? — then he would certainly include fancy weaved brackets beneath the eaves. Pigeons were kept away by well placed whirling pinwheels or perhaps by a watchful cat concealed within one of the many ducts beneath the high-pitched roof.

The turreted Crocker mansion quickly became a landmark on South Olive Street. Even during early misty mornings the open verandas were still visible from Hill and Third Streets below. The three story house had the look of a mocking gothic castle, guarded by the soaring tower in the east wing. Two gables and a small balcony set into the roof added to its regal prominence.

It was during this time that one of the leading merchants of Los Angeles decided to construct a showplace on top of the Hill which would be long remembered. F. F. Coulter imported glass for his crystal windows and he was insured of a near-perfect view of the rising sun each morning.

Further along the crest, Pedro Larronde built his "castle in the sky" at 237 South Hope Street. The Spanish influence was beginning to take form and this was later to integrate into the architectural plans of the future home buyers on the Hill.

The Hill was beginning to show signs of solidarity in the early times of 1890. Here is an excellent, clear view of Temple and Broadway toward Hill Street. The roads look a little rough (some are yet to be paved), but the residences appear well-kept and ready for inspection.

There was one man who never lived on the Hill but had more to do with its continued existence than anyone else. Colonel J. W. Eddy was a personal friend of Abraham Lincoln and actually campaigned for him during the Presidential elections of 1860. He was an engineer by profession and was closely associated with the building of railroads.

In 1895 he came to southern California to survey the proposed transmission line that would bring power from Kern to Los Angeles. It was as though Fate had decided this was the right moment for his arrival into this area. The new City Hall was being built on Broadway just east of Bunker Hill and a certain uncomfortable congestion was beginning to take place.

At this time there was no public transportation up the side of the Hill. Plans had been proposed for a cable line to reach Second Street, but were later rejected because the incline was too steep. Fear of possible serious accidents made this move impractical. Satirical cartoons were even drawn to illustrate the mishaps which could take place.

No politician or engineer wanted to be personally involved in such a possible catastrophe. It could wipe out their career with a single stroke.

Colonel Eddy, however, was his own man. In the past he had operated so-called impossible ventures and sometimes come through with his head above water. Now he was moved to throw his hat in a troubled ring once more.

On May 10, 1901, he petitioned the Los Angeles City Council for a franchise to operate an electric cable railway to travel over the Third Street right-of-way from Hill to Olive Street. His suggestion was looked upon as madness by some. There was even a hint that the Colonel was only proposing this to the Council for personal publicity. He really had no intention of carrying out his plans at all.

The Colonel was 69 at the time and was in no mood to play games. He was absolutely serious and made this clear to all concerned. Ten days later he received his questionable franchise. Mayor M. P. Snyder signed the agreement authorizing the construction and now it was all up to the indefatigable Colonel to get the work done.

Within six months the railway was officially opened. Punch was served at both ends of the line. It wasn't alcoholic because they didn't want to encourage any accidents on the first day.

Over 2,000 passengers made the trip on the inaugural journey. No fee was charged although donations were subtly requested. The original cars seated only ten passengers and were open to the air. It all depended upon the condition of the weather as to where was the best place to sit. There were times when the rain would slant inside and the knowledgeable rider always brought along sheets of heavy translucent paper to protect himself from the inclement weather.

No one knows whose decision it was to have the exterior painted a spotless white. It might have been that they secretly desired a saintly look for the moving carriages. Or perhaps they hoped that the sun would reflect on these wooden panels and visitors from afar would wonder and marvel at their flight up into the distant environs and gladly become paying customers.

The time of christening of these small cars is unknown also but they did receive the names "Olivet" and "Sinai" on the day of their first journey. It has been recorded that certain superstitious people would purposely wait until "their car" arrived at the station below. One name had five letters, the other six. If you were a serious student of numerology then this pertinent information could have lasting meaning to you.

It is sad to report that the name of the first operator has been lost in the bureaucratic filing system of the past. He was a man of great importance for it was his hand and judgment which regulated the speed and constancy of the Angel's Flight. He sat near the engine room at the top and with an eagle's view of the platform down below personally made the decision when the cars should start in motion.

It was not only the prosperous residents who made these daily trips up the Hill, there was also the cooks, butlers, chauffeurs, gardeners, and men and women for all occasions who were needed for the continuity of such an affluent lifestyle.

About the start of the twentieth century, hotels became big business on top of the Hill. Formal houses such as the Melrose advertised extensively and one could command a fashionable room overlooking the city for the remarkable sum of $2.00. (These were the days when an accommodation at San Diego's deluxe Hotel Coronado was $2.50 a

Construction halted a number of times on the E. P. Bryan home at 333 S. Grand Avenue, as changes in the architectural plans were made without warning. It was understood that Mr. Bryan had a superstitious nature. Count the steps leading to the first landing and then the ones up to the porch. The first group adds up to 14, the second to 12. Thirteen was a number that was not to be associated with this address in any way! Even the triple three's in the street number had special mystical significance.

day — including meals!)

The Belmont, at the terminus of the Second Street Cable Railway, featured broad verandas where the tired salesmen could sit during the dusk hours and observe the modish carriages ride by. After awhile the identifying marks of each conveyance could be quickly identified and a possible destination surmised. These conjectures could be compared later to the final results if such information became available from the Bunker Hill gossip circle.

Some hotels were only known by the name of the owner themselves. Mrs. Henrietta Tucker had ten rooms and would meet her guests personally at the door. Some of her visitors would stay for months or even years at a time. The price was certainly reasonable enough with the top fare around one dollar a day.

Mayor Snyder (right) at the La Fiesta de Los Angeles with President Theodore Roosevelt in 1903 was most conscious of the right kind of publicity at all times. He made sure he was at the honored table with the chief executive on this particular visit. It was said that the only time he really took a chance with his untarnished political image was when he signed an agreement with Colonel Eddy authorizing the construction of the smallest railroad in the world up the side of Bunker Hill. There was a very good chance this might have been known as Snyder's Folly!

The cable cars didn't last in Los Angeles as they did in San Francisco. An attempt was made to carry these colorful cars right up the side of Bunker Hill, but the strain was too much. Maybe this was one reason they were soon dismantled for other forms of transportation. In the picture below one of these sturdy vehicles comes to a smooth stop at the corner of Second Street and Broadway.

Then there was the John T. LaDu residence hotel. During the convention months, every one of his 32 rooms was filled. A bible was supplied to each paying guest and on some of the pages were later found words of praise for the service offered them during their brief stay.

One of the goliaths of its time was the 67-unit hotel on the corner of First and Hope Streets. The Dome was immediately identifiable by its Turkish-style turret which squatted down evenly over its red tile roof. More than mere overnight rooms were offered in this imperial establishment. The quasi-atmosphere of Mission-styled comfort was guaranteed with each registration.

During the baronial days of the Hill, the hotels that were clustered together kept themselves like pampered ladies of the court. A structure like the Lovejoy Apartments on Third Street went to great pains to be distinguished from all sides. No matter on what angle a visitor might suddenly appear he would be immediately impressed — at least momentarily — by the glowing plaster garlands that encompassed the lower floors of the rectangular building.

Busy executives from out of town were beginning to become aware of the Hill's unique accommodations. Often the Royal Building, 300 South Olive Street, would be included in their itinerary. Boxing matches were regularly held in the small adjoining gymnasium and although no one really famous ever appeared in this ring, the activity was fast and furious enough to make a Saturday evening intriguing to lonely businessmen looking for some offbeat divertisement.

It was not the purpose of the Bunker Hill region to encourage industry of any kind and yet a peculiar type of "business" did spring up which might have been more successful if the entrepreneurs had been more serious.

A carrier pigeon service between Bunker Hill and Catalina Island was started by Otto and Hector Zahn, with the help of Mac Casenave, a cousin of Ana Begue de Packman. The birds were primarily sent to young ladies who had been most friendly in the summertime, and this was a convenient way of continuing the relationship.

It was entirely possible that other messages could have been sent to traveling salesmen during these times of slow and inefficient mail service. The boys were only interested in getting quick responses from their girlfriends and the idea of combining their activities with a business schedule didn't appeal to them at all.

Judge Anson Brunson, builder of a three-story mansion in the center of Bunker Hill, was known for his terrible temper in court. Without warning he would lift his voice and command attention. These outbursts gave him a reputation for being highly unpredictable. He was just the opposite when he returned to his beautiful home on the Hill. It was as though he were living two lives, and neither one would ever come in contact with the other.

There was no denying that it took money to live up on the Hill. No one discussed their personal financial situation and yet when a monetary setback did occur, all were aware of it.

A classic example of this involved a lady by the name of Mrs. Anson Brunson, wife of Judge Brunson, an early law partner of Henry O'Melveny. It was inevitable that their spacious mansion should become a meeting place for the social elite. The very structure of their house invited large distinguished gatherings.

Their residence on Grand, just a little bit north of Fourth Street, had an immense drawing room over 60 feet long. Antiques were wheeled up the side of the Hill in padded crates and Mrs. Brunson personally inspected the ritual unpacking.

Many important business deals were made in that paneled library, and the judge proved to be as much an amiable host as his charming and

The unique architectural style of the Larronde Pierre mansion at 237 N. Hope Street caused a number of writers to speculate as to where the owner received his inspiration. The dome projecting from the east wing of the house could well accommodate a park band if it were closer to the foundation.

gracious wife. Then with apparently little warning a financial crisis crashed through these placid walls. The accustomed fashionable life came to an abrupt end. Others on the Hill were remotely aware of what was happening, but their own modish lifestyle continued along without abatement. It was much like observing a sinking ship on the horizon. There was no way help could be offered without possibly scuttling their own fragile vessel.

It can not be assumed that the residents of the early Bunker Hill were heartless, mercenary souls who lived only by a set of inflexible rules for survival. There was no way possible that the Hill residents could pool their resources, nor was this at all ever suggested.

Mrs. Randolph Huntington Minor from San Francisco created the first Los Angeles Blue Book of society and the names which were submitted to her had to be impeccable.

If financial difficulties were forcing certain important social cutbacks, then these unfortunate

conditions could be reflected in the published listings in the Los Angeles 400. Little has changed as far as the upper echelon is concerned. You either make it big or forget about living on top of the Hill.

Other structures besides elegant mansions were being erected on the Hill during those early epic days. The builder of the Angel's Flight decided to raise an unusual edifice near the Olive Street entrance. In his mind was a continued glorification of the small independent railway.

Before the very eyes of the amazed residents down below he constructed a 100-foot steel observation tower near the crest. To some it looked as though it would topple down the Hill with the first decent strong wind. The Colonel knew exactly what he was doing and summarily ignored all the critics.

To give his beloved tower an even more magical touch he equipped the rectangular cabin on top with a camera obscura and those who entered the darkened room would be given a strange illuminated view of the moving city down below.

The size and shape of the little railway itself was gradually changing with the times. In the beginning the track ran at ground level, then was reconstructed to a uniform 33 per cent grade on wooden trestles.

No one considered the possibility of rot in those halcyon days of slow speeds and quieter times. As the city became more mechanized and human natures began to harden, it would seem only natural that the soft timbers of the past would be replaced with reinforced concrete frames that would forever ignore the rays of the California sun.

The angle of the Angel was always being subtly adjusted. Consulting engineers decided that ground level was no longer practical. The first 50 feet now became a filled ramp and the final 55 feet were laid directly on the steep hillside.

More power was allocated to the motor located at the top of the Hill. Perhaps America was beginning to get fat and more effort was needed to pull them to the next plateau.

A top speed of 720 rpm was now possible. More safety was being stressed and a seven-eighths of an inch steel crucible cable held onto those little cars with more power never before believed possible. The breaking strength was tested at 52,000 pounds, which was considered more than enough for the traffic expected.

There was always the nervous rider, however,

In 1902 the Third Street tunnel was in operation and being serviced by an electric streetcar. Modern times were coming to the residents of Bunker Hill, and only greater happenings were predicted for this fashionable area. Building was at its peak this year, and the Angel's Flight had been traveling up and down its steel path for more than a year.

who would sometimes inquire as to the braking capacity of the four mile an hour cars. The patient operator had his standard answer ready: a bronze wedge served as an emergency brake. This not only halted the movement of the pulley but also forced the cable to the bottom of the groove beneath the tracks where it could be quickly jammed. If a cable should suddenly break for some unknown reason, then the other half would be instantly secured and at least one of the moving cars would be stopped in its tracks.

Meanwhile, the top of the Hill was experiencing its own kind of adjustment. Time was passing without regard to honored tradition. The posh mansions were becoming out of style. Industry was pushing its way into the city blocks down below.

As a sign of impatience and material contempt for Bunker Hill's architectural esthetics, two tunnels were forged directly through the very core of the beloved crest. The Third Street tunnel was completed at the incredible cost of $103,958 which included all labor and materials. And then several years later the Hill tunnel was officially opened for the convenience of the increased traffic.

These excavations were becoming costly and the omnipotent minds of the City Council decided that giant cuts through the Hill was the most practical action to take. This meant drastically slicing up the Hill at First and Second Street. Suddenly the costs were doubled and then doubled again! The estimate was $4,000,000. Screams of protest were heard from both the flatland to the crest of Olive Street.

For the first time the local businessmen and the residents of the Hill combined their efforts to halt an unwanted change coming to Bunker Hill. Each had their own reason, but this didn't make any

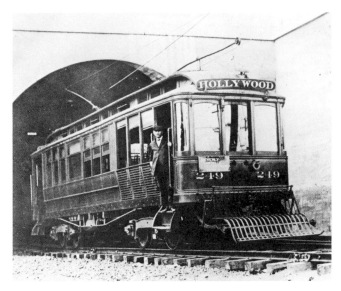

The first street car through the new Hill Street tunnel shown on September 23, 1909. It was easier to go through Bunker Hill than over it.

In 1915 the City Council decided to make two giant cuts through the Hill at a cost of about $4 million. Naturally taxes would have to be raised to allow for these expenditures, and this caused immediate protests from citizens and a number of downtown businessmen. The power of an outraged public paid off for once; a compromise was reached. The cuts were abandoned and First Street was graded instead. A tunnel was substituted for a cut at Second Street and was not completed until 1924. The picture below is an intermediate construction shot of the Second Street tunnel.

difference; for the moment they were advocates of the same cause.

This fight frankly surprised the politicians. They thought everyone except perhaps a small minority would agree with their proposals. They were not ready for the daily barrage which occurred from the moment of the first announcement.

Since they did want to stay in office for another term — and hopefully also beyond that. — they finally backed off and decided instead to grade First Street down so that access to that section of town would not be so difficult. Another tunnel was substituted for a cut at Second Street, and this made a total of three giant holes through the tender bowels of Bunker Hill so far.

Although the victory banner waved high on the crest the night of these partial triumphs, there were other clever anarchists waiting in the wings to offer their particular battle plans for the extinction of Bunker Hill.

All this constant attrition was progressively breaking down the social clique which had once ruled the Hill. Families were moving away to less entrenched areas.

At one time the Berke mansion on the northwest corner of Second Street and Bunker Hill had the laudable reputation for gaiety and social camaraderie. This beautiful three story structure was built by Ferdinand Berke in 1810 and the family enjoyed the glories of this magnificent dwelling for many decades.

Generations of Berkes came to know this one address as their home. And then the time arrived when it was all over. Furniture was moved out and a general decay began to attack the foundation. The house was not entirely deserted, but later taken over by a Mr. Anderson. He saw other possibilities in this rambling old mansion.

With a few structural adjustments here and there, the former elite residence could easily be turned into a serviceable rooming house for transients in the neighborhood. Nothing cheap was contemplated at the time; it would only be a necessary convenience for those on the move.

Soon many of the fabled mansions on the Hill would play host to passing strangers. Some were kinder than others and traveled through without etching their initials or words of praise or disgust on the once polished curved banisters.

Parties would still be given beneath those vaulted ceilings, only the beverage was apt to be beer and wine rather than the vintage champagne of old. Change had indeed taken place within these once venerated walls but the foundation was still firmly in place and to think that one day that too would vanish was a ridiculous speculation.

Years later when the bloodless bulldozers began their insidious push to the boundary lines, Mr. Anderson was forced to vacate the premises and move to a two-story house across the way.

From the bedroom window of his new home he could easily observe the wrecking process and one can only imagine his emotions at that time. Although he was not the original owner, he had certainly experienced the warmth and cordiality of the old Berke mansion.

If the spirits of men do occupy their former abodes for a certain length of time before passing over to that other sphere of eternal reality, then Ferdinand Berke must have also been a bewildered observer of these calamitous times.

Why should any civilized society think of tearing down a structure which had once been hailed as an architectural triumph? What could possibly replace the grandeur of a time in history when the pace was leisurely and the idea that man could control the forces of nature were thought to be both blasphemous and impractical.

A year before the Great Depression, another formidable enemy of the Hill appeared on the scene and he was an individual of great action and purpose. C. C. Bigelow believed fervently that he had finally solved the problem of that big hump of dirt looming up in the middle of a thriving downtown Los Angeles. His solution was direct and simple: "Level it! Right down to the Hill Street grade!" As incredible as this sounded at the time he actually had a very practical approach to his proposition.

Using hydraulic pressure equipment similar to those employed in mining, the work could be

New transportation buildings had to be constructed to take care of the expanding population in Los Angeles in the early 1920s. During this same time Bunker Hill was experiencing its greatest building boom, and the residents were assured of direct routes to almost any part of the city by the Pacific Electric.

The steel framework of the Southern California Edison building at the corner of Fifth and Grand on Bunker Hill was almost completed in 1930. For the moment this would be the largest structure on the Hill.

This was the scene on the southwest side of Bunker Hill just before the big depression of 1929 hit the country. The Sherwood and Zelda Apartments were still in operation on Grand Avenue. Inside parking was the huge sum of $10 a month, and construction was beginning on the new Edison building. Through it all the Engstrum Hotel remained the same indomitable landmark it is today.

accomplished in surprisingly little time. The contoured lots would soon be pulpy mounds of inky mud. Trucks would be backed up for blocks to carry away the residue of a lifestyle that had to be destroyed before progress could possibly advance.

Once more the costs for mutilating the Bunker Hill region increased to an improbable height. No one was ready for the final amount which in those days was positively staggering.

For $50 million the Bigelow operation could be completed and in a very short time this Hill of contention would be wiped away forever.

Opponents on both sides of the question were lining up for another vicious fight. The City Council was once more in the middle, and from this comfortable position they employed engineer William H. Babcock to further develop this plan of removal. In a little less than three years his survey was completed. Bigelow had to forget about his hydraulic pressure equipment; the new way stressed a regrading project.

When the papers carried the story about these proposed plans, the banners of rebellion began to wave once more. Imagine chopping off the crown of picturesque Bunker Hill. That would be like decapitating Venus de Milo so she would fit inside a smaller museum.

The only palatable part of the entire suggestion was possibly the reduced cost of operation. The regrading would run about half as much as the original Bigelow plan. Even so, no one on top of the Hill was looking for bargains like this. Again this was a fight for survival and the hot blood was racing from Temple to Fifth Street and back again.

Although the City Council pushed for the passage of this proposal, the majority of the public would have nothing to do with it. Bigelow finally had to admit that the human equation was too much to fight. In 1938 the City Council issued its final news release on the subject. They were willing to allow "the natural force of economics to do the job." Everyone had their own dire interpretation of that brief comment to the press.

Even though the general area of Bunker Hill was allowed to remain basically the same during these fierce confrontations, all those intimately involved in the political and financial manuevers knew it was only a matter of time before this quaint area would soon fade away.

To keep some kind of tangible evidence of this quiet time and place in history, a group of un-

It was tragic to view the gradual decline of the beautiful old proud mansions of Bunker Hill. The home of Judge Brousseau withstood the elements for a number of years, but finally succumbed to the ravages of time. In this picture we see rampaging weeds instead of the once well-kept lawns. The wooden banisters look as though they might collapse from a sudden gust of wind, and the upstairs has a sinister, desolate look that would fit well into a tale of mystery and suspense.

employed draftsmen were hired by the WPA to create a topographical map of this area. They worked at ground level to construct the miniatures of the hotels and private residence still standing on the narrow streets.

In another three years the depression was going to come to an abrupt halt. The Second World War put everyone back to work — even some of the perennial welfare recipients who were now living permanently on top of the Hill.

Before that time of December, 1941, when news of Pearl Harbor swept the country, a seemingly inconsequential incident happened concerning the rules in the downtown fire district.

New buildings had always been required to have masonry walls. Accordingly the old rooming houses on the Hill weren't giving way to new buildings. The City Council decided to change the fire district for most of the hilltop region and

This scale-model scene of Bunker Hill and environs was the result of many months of objective viewing by a group of dedicated WPA draftsmen during the late 1930 s. They took their lunches with them, and sometimes sat on one of the porches they were scaling down at the moment. Some residents treated them as intruders, or even worse, as indifferent recorders preparing for a future Armageddon on the Hill.

allow stucco-type apartments. From the ruling it was hoped that builders would be encouraged to construct new dwellings in some of the deteriorated areas. No one realized at that particular moment that there wasn't any more time. The country would soon be at war and thoughts of regional interest had to be submerged for those of national importance.

Men and women who would never have visited the Los Angeles area if it had not been for the war were now introduced to the Bunker Hill area via that little railway which was still industrially climbing the same side of the same hill.

Inflation had not yet hit the Angel's Flight. The charge was five cents a ride or a block of six tickets for 25 cents. There was even a special souvenir booklet containing 24 tickets for only a dollar.

The cars were now making as many as 400 trips a day. Someone noted at this time that the Flight was chartered as a railroad by the State of California, even so it had to be considered a non-scheduled line. The first flight would always take-off promptly at 6:00 a.m. and the last run would be 18 hours later at 12:20 a.m.

If many of the oldtime residents of the Hill could have returned during these unsettled times, they would have been astounded by the sights which would have greeted them.

The grounds where once the resolute Judge Widney and his lovely wife held court for the beautiful people of their time was now a low-priced parking lot. Further down the road was another even more traumatic shock for a former resident. The two-story mansion of Colonel Bradbury, which once looked down upon the entire city of Los Angeles from the corner of Court and Hill, was now nothing but a hole in the ground. A seismic catastrophe could not have been more devastating to his well-kept grounds.

At the conclusion of the war, it seemed only natural to establish another bureaucratic office to somehow straighten out the mess which had taken place on top of the Hill mainly because of bureaucratic interference in the past.

This is not exactly a fair way of introducing the Community Redevelopment Agency, but the residents who were still holding fast on the brink of this wobbling crest were in no mood to be kind to anyone. They knew their time was limited and they were determined to be as angry and as aggressive as possible at all times.

The bond issue which was to provide a revolving fund for the redevelopment of Bunker Hill didn't get a two-thirds majority and the Agency was momentarily stymied. By now the oldtimers were weak and weary from all the former fights. They needed a time to breathe, and little was to be given to them.

A new county courthouse was in the active planning stage. Adjoining that area would be the city Water and Power Department buildings. These structures would need a lot of space, and of course the Hill was the only visible obstruction at the time.

A new breed of pioneers appeared on the scene in the late forties. They were peripatetic artists who were determined to capture the essence of the old neighborhood before the wreckers were given full leeway.

It wasn't uncommon for two or three artists to be "working" on the same location. Sometimes the colorful inhabitants of the building would offer their services for a price. Someone sitting on a wide veranda gave the scene a look of false promise for the future.

Artists like Ben Abril painted on location because of the excitement generated by proximity. All that stood before him at that moment would soon be gone. Like an early morning dream which had only a few furtive breaths left, the old Bunker Hill would soon be fragmented memories and swatches of paint on a canvas.

If someone with a great deal of money had been clairvoyant during those early times around 1860, there is little doubt that they would have made a fortune.

The value of land in certain sections of Los Angeles increased at an incredible rate during the coming decades. A corner of Main Street could have been purchased for $300 a front foot. Less than ten years later it went up to $500 and then doubled that in the next decade. Lands four miles

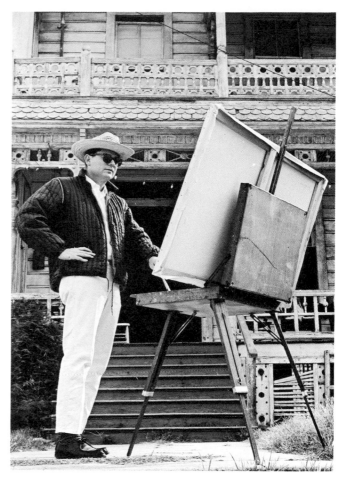

Traveling artists set up their equipment on location in an attempt to capture some of the fading glory of Bunker Hill. At this point (1952) the old Judge Brousseau mansion had become a transient rooming house, and the gingerbread ornaments were becoming stale and brittle. No attempt was ever made to rejuvenate these classic homes; only certain involved artists took the time to permanently record their existence on canvas.

outside the city limits of Los Angeles that were sold for $1 an acre in 1868 catapulted up to $1,000 an acre.

The historic houses on top of Bunker Hill were not important to the developers. They wanted the land and it had to be flat enough for the highrisers and condominiums they had in mind.

Once the Harbor Freeway made its tumescent concrete arc along the Hill's western base this was the beginning of the end for this aesthetic sanctuary.

There was even talk that the beloved Angel's Flight would be eliminated. No one in the area could take this kind of loose talk serious. The

Suddenly and without warning, a deadly fire rushed along these narrow corridors of the Dome hotel on top of Bunker Hill during the summer of 1964. Since the stairways were open to the very top floor, there were no obstructions to retard the killer blaze.

line had to be drawn somewhere. How would the pensioners get down to the Grand Central Market at the bottom of the Hill? Who would carry the cripple and sick down to Pershing Square where they could challenge anyone in sight to a game of checkers or chess? These were serious questions which could not be ignored.

It would be too much to ask any of them to walk those long flights of stairs. No, the Angel's Flight could never go. It was more than a memory of a glorious past; it still had a viable purpose in life and its destruction would be senseless — or at least these were the thoughts for the moment.

By now the Community Redevelopment Agency was moving along with more dominant authority. Property was acquired lot by lot much like an expert chess player would move across the guarded spaces held by his inexperienced opponent. Objects still filtered out from some of the old-time residents. No longer were their angry protestations newsworthy. They seemed like feeble gestures from meaningless phantoms who should have faded away long ago.

Once more an incident occurred which speeded up the so-called urban renewal of the Hill. Late

in July, 1964 a fire started on the first floor of the old Dome Hotel. Within minutes the entire structure was aflame. The narrow corridors made it difficult — and in some cases impossible — for the elderly occupants to reach either a door or a window.

Fire trucks and equipment had to climb the steep Hill and crowd into the congested streets. By now the top of the crest was thick with billowing smoke. From miles around the blaze could be observed and perhaps at that moment some of the oldtimers who had since moved away shook their heads knowing that one more terrible calamity had hit their old familiar homestead.

The next morning the papers carried the complete details of the misfortune. Six had been injured and one killed. These statistics were enough to create the necessary protest to level the remaining old Bunker Hill structures.

The emotions of the moment cancelled out any reasonable thought. Soon temporary parking lots would cover most of the top of the Hill. The dilapidated rooming houses would be cut down as though they were malignant weeds.

All thoughts of renovating these old classic buildings were immediately dismissed by those in authority. There wasn't time. Progress was pushing in on all sides with a vengeance. Those who dared opposed her drive would surely be destroyed themselves. And who in any high place would willingly go against the tide of conversion?

Thankfully none of the old residents were witnesses to the slow decomposition of the neighborhood. It would have surely struck Judge Brousseau down if he had been able to return in another couple of decades and seen strange people entering and leaving his stately mansion without notice. He would never have understood that his private dwelling was now merely one more of the many rooming houses spotted across the Hill. None of the guests were asked for references; all that was needed was the first week's rent and then the key was offered without question.

The Judge would have been even more amazed if he had seen the strange vehicle parked in front of his house. His eyes would have blinked a number of times until they fully registered the shape and color of the oblong conveyance. It was a deserted bus! Right on the front lawn. What would the gardner have thought if he had come by at that moment to clip the regimented hedge?

Probably it would have been too much for the Judge to also realize that someone was actually living in this old rusting bus. It was, of course, illegal but this was overlooked by the authorities at the time since this kind of lifestyle seemed to fit in so well with the current etiquette observed on top of the Hill.

In an attempt to save some of the venerable landmarks of the Hill, one of the old mansions was moved off its ancient mooring and settled on to a new foundation miles away from the menacing bulldozers.

On October 30, 1959, the two-story structure at 325 Bunker Hill Avenue was hoisted upon a network of steel girders and carefully edged down the side of the Hill for a long, slow trip to the Arroyo Seco Park in Pasadena.

Some observers thought the old place would never make it. It had taken too many jolts and disappointments in the past and this final shove away from its birthplace would collapse whatever spirit it had left.

The doubters were all wrong! All walls and hand painted ceilings were intact as the movers finally rolled away. Hiding in the shadows, however, was another menace which no one had considered before. Vandals were eagerly waiting to break the streaked glass windows and light fires beneath the dry timbers. This journey to safety had really been a death march. Nothing remained except a few of the metal door hinges and some smoldering window frames which still carried vestiges of dampness from the side of the Hill.

The Mission Apartments on the corner of Second and Olive had the same kind of painful

Trying to save the past is sometimes a thankless job. This residence at 339 S. Bunker Hill Avenue was taken down the side of the Hill at great expense on December 7, 1968. The curious lady gazing up at the notice for removal looks as though she were somewhat perplexed that the city would pay this much for such a dilapidated structure.

A terrible loneliness overshadowed the occupants of the old rooming houses on the Hill in the 1950s. It was generally understood that all structures in the immediate vicinity would soon be razed. The lack of permanency in life was vividly demonstrated every day on these quiet avenues of Bunker Hill.

falling from grace. The indifferent tenants would often hang their washing out on the roof. From below, the shabby building looked as though it were a waterlogged tanker docking for the very last time.

Finally a full parcel of land within the 136-acre Bunker Hill Project was offered for sale. The Connecticut General Life Insurance Company came up with the highest bid and also the plans for the tallest building in Los Angeles at that time.

Within the block bordered by the Harbor Freeway and Fourth Street, Figueroa, and Fifth Streets, a 42-story office tower was going to be constructed. Lady McDonald and her magic hydraulic elevator would have both been astounded at the noiseless contrivances which could now whisk people thousands of feet up in the air.

Two incisive words were injected into the overall design for the conversion of Hill property: all future plans would ultimately orbit around "traffic circulation." The automobile was king! Freeways had proven that the combustible engine needed straight uninterrupted thoroughfares to be efficient.

Looking back on some of the devices which were employed to erase Bunker Hill from the pages of official records, it would appear that all the bureaucratic offices got together at one time to harass the forlorn neighborhood into the ground.

The Los Angeles Police Department called the Hill "a high frequency crime area." They said that several of the apartment houses catered to known moral offenders.

Next the Health Department offered its closely tabulated survey. According to these statistics, the prevalence of active tuberculosis on the Hill was approximately three times that of the flat-lands down below.

Was it the mild elevation that was causing this unseemly epidemic? Or was it the unhealthy tensions that were perpetrated on the hapless owners and renters on top of the Hill?

The Fire Department continued to issue warnings of doom to all who would risk their lives by continuing to live in the unsafe dwellings. During one publicized tour, they discovered a number of "six and seven story frame apartment buildings with inadequate exits."

Later the report from the Los Angeles Community Redevelopment Agency truly revealed the reason for this uncommon pressure for change in this one neighborhood of Los Angeles.

In the early 1950s, the total assessed value of the Bunker Hill region was a little under $5 million. If the Agency's proposed project of height limit for apartment house, a realignment of the streets and some regrading of the hilltop went through, it would increase the value to over $30 million.

The annual tax revenue would then be increased from the present $332,000 to over $2 million. That was a lot of money to slip through your fingers just because a few so-called quaint houses were considered historic landmarks and the people who occupied them characters from another time.

The City Tax Agency was moved to announce that "the Bunker Hill area didn't even come close to paying for the governmental services that were provided for it!"

Eight thousand people lived on the Hill which made it almost a small town. Unfortunately it wasn't independent enough to fight against all these powerful negative attacks. The transients had continual personal troubles of their own. Many of the buildings were operated under absentee ownerships. The landlord might be living in San Francisco and got most of his news concerning the Hill second hand, if at all.

The few who still had private homes along the narrow streets lived in a strange admixture of fear and bewilderment. The environment around them was in a bubbling vortex of senseless alteration. The cordial neighbors of the past were nowhere to be seen. The proud mansions which had once been filled with laughing familiar voices now had sullen strangers wandering about the unkept grounds. Their eyes would betray the dark indifference within them. They cared not at all for the future of this old Hill for it was only a brief stopping off point between one aimless day and another.

Once the honored vanguard of the past was no longer able to stand at attention, the drawbridges of the Bunker Hill castles of long ago were extremely vulnerable. The enemy scouts who could be public officials in disguise might pass over at any time and without warning rip out the supports which have kept these lofty pavilions suspended in a quiet reality for many decades and tumble them down the soft slopes of the Hill into the mechanized whirlpool below.

When the courts gave the Community Redevelopment Agency the right to start buying property up on the Hill the dam broke loose against this tight little bastion of individuality.

The first "earthquake-proof" building on the Hill belonged to the Sunkist people. The seven-story structure with an elevated penthouse was designed by Walker & Eisen and was the art deco sensation of Los Angeles when unveiled in September, 1935. Harold Wilson designed the molden bas-reliefs on the front, which were unfortunately destroyed with the rest of the building later. It took 19 million pounds of concrete and 750,000 tons of steel to put it all together. The land went for the bargain price of $117,000, and the building cost a mere $365,000.

A new kind of power had been unleashed that at first completely baffled the property owners who were under seige. They couldn't imagine that any government agency would ever have the power to uproot them from their homes. On a cool May morning of 1961 they discovered that such an awesome authority did indeed exist.

Within a few months the CRA bought its first land parcel which contained 23 units with the same amount of elderly inhabitants still on the premises.

These people are not identifiable now and yet the fear which they must have experienced at that time must have been electrifying. They were more alone in the world than they had ever been before. No longer were there organized groups to fight against this upheaval on top of the Hill. The courts and the community down below had deserted them. They must move on regardless of their emotional attachment to the house and property that had been a part of their lives for so very long.

The first building to be demolished under the new law was the five-story Hillcrest Hotel, built

33

The builders were moving fast in the late 1950s. Already an excavation stands next to the foundation of the old Berke mansion on the northwest corner of Second Street and Bunker Hill. The transients living on the premises had to be careful on their return home at night. The lack of adequate street lighting made the nearby walk perilous.

in the resplendent times of 1904 and located on South Olive Street near the Angel's Flight upper station.

Under the law the agency had to find comparable housing for the 50 tenants before the structure could be torn down. But where did such agreeable tranquility exist? All about them was surging progress. Since the 13-story height limit had been made void, the race to see who could build the tallest building in Los Angeles continued at an unrelenting speed.

The law also required CRA to follow up on its relocation work. Unfortunately these specific records are closed to the public. Is it possible that the results were far from satisfactory, at least from the humane point of view? Can we uproot Man from a discovered place of tranquility and place him in a convenient cubicle where he may eat, sleep and work like the thousands of others about him and feel he will forever — or at least three score and ten — be satisfied with his lot? Is this the heritage he will remember and treasure in his heart?

While public attention was centered primarily on top of the Hill another kind of change was taking place on one of the nearby slopes. It is natural to condense time like this when an old friend passes away. You think only of the moment

of transition, not the continuity of why or how it happened.

On a hot summer day in May, 1969, a lot of people who really didn't know each other gathered around a wooden archway on Hill Street. Some started to cry because they were older and had more memories stored away. The younger ones didn't look at them in contempt because they instinctively knew that one day they too would have some precious recollection swept away from them for no other reason than it was too old to exist in the present time with compatibility.

The Angel's Flight was going to be torn down! From the gradual wearing down of the Hill, the old cars and equipment no longer met the engineering and safety standards. The small vehicles had been ever-faithful for over six decades and were more than willing to continue on with that enviable record. Modern progress was indifferent to fidelity. Only strict utilitarianism works.

To protect some of the material wealth of the continually disappearing Hill, the Cultural Heritage Board promptly declared Angel's Flight a historic-cultural monument. This didn't mean that someone couldn't rip it up from its roots and bundle it up into a nearby closet like an unwanted birthday present. The announcement only insured against its public destruction.

The cars were lifted off the 300-foot track and carefully dropped on waiting trucks. They were about to take their last ride due west. No mournful procession followed the moving caravan because this was not to be considered a death but rather a carefully planned rejuvenation.

The Community Redevelopment Agency promised all those who had written and called in about the destiny of this block long funicular that the Angel's Flight would once more come alive sometime in the future. No exact date could be given because no one knew for sure when the so-called redevelopment of Bunker Hill would take place.

The final resting place for the shortest railway in the world was predicted by a number of newspapermen of the time. Some suggested that the Flight would end up at Travel Town in Griffith Park. Here small children of all ages could once more experience the adventure of watching two cars pass by each other as though they were mystical wood and metal blood brothers.

Then there was the Hollywood Bowl. The elevation would be just right and the crowds who would come to listen to the concerts could for

*The remains of the glorious Angel's Flight now are tucked
away in an old warehouse on the south side of Los Angeles.
Decay and dirt don't completely cover the glory of these
vintage cars. They still proudly proclaim that they were
once the only dependable transportation to the top of the
Hill.*

One of the truly heart-rending sights of life is to see an old friend discarded and forgotten — but so it happened to the Angel's Flight when it made its last journey to a warehouse off 24th Street and Hoover in Los Angeles. The fares are still visible on the slanting front of the car (below), but the windows look as though they were pulling back and attempting to run in the opposite direction. Escape while you can! But too late. Too late. Inside one of the cars (left) a workman stands near an exit. From this angle the streets look almost normal. If a buzzer should suddenly sound, one might instinctively reach out to balance himself as the car began its magical climb to the top of the Hill once more.

a brief moment forget about the congestion of the parking lots and climb the side of the hill like a genuine noblesse from the past.

All the guesses were wrong. The cars were eventually dumped in the middle of a concrete structure off 24th Street and Hoover which had once been a thriving laundry. In this uncomely building, along with deserted water heaters, electrical pumps, and other assorted rusting mechanical devices, "Olivet" and "Sinai" were placed together like two lovers in a suicidal tryst.

The final purchase price for the Angel's Flight was $35,000. The old deteriorating cars weren't worth that much at all. The paint was all peeling and the seats were much too dirty. Perhaps part of that money was for the thousands of memories which still traversed those sad ramshackle frames.

Once the moving cars on the side of the Hill were safely tucked away, the bulldozers moved with more certainty. What was once a deteriorative garden district elevated above the city of Los Angeles now became a sterile flat acreage.

Parking lots piled on top of one another and the trip across Grand to Fourth Street had to be made without stop. Signs along the way warned any curious driver who might like to park for a moment and gaze across the empty lots towards the deserted concrete abutments to continue on without looking from one side to the other.

A lone tree rests at the crest of the Hill, leaning towards the Central Market down below. On the bark are etched initials made by heretical youth who care only to leave their personal mark on some still standing form of nature resting midst the lonely tomb of Bunker Hill.

Dirt trails lead from one mound to another, and if these are traveled during the daylight hours no one will usually be advancing in the opposite direction. At night the derelicts up from Hill Street amble along scouting for places to sleep or perhaps to drink their bottle of cheap wine in peace and quiet.

Standing near the center of one of these open fields you can easily imagine yourself somehow separated from the rush of traffic on the streets on either side.

The empty concrete shell which once housed the colorful Angel's Flight has no romantic nostalgia to it, nor is the mind enticed to conjure up those moments of long ago. There is that same feeling that the occupants of old Bunker Hill had years ago. None of this will ever change, the permanency of the weed-ridden lots looks absolute.

The only remaining sign of a time that can never return floats before the U.S. Post Office at the very foot of the old Bunker Hill region — One Bunker Hill. Farther up the Hill only parking lots and empty spaces are its vapid neighbors. And if you're one who remembers the Golden Days, then it would hardly pay to stop off and mail even a postcard to a friend back home.

Once more the illusion of status quo blinds the eye. The truth that nothing stays the same is an abstraction too difficult to integrate into the mind.

Only paper plans presently foretell the future of Bunker Hill. The Urban Renewal Project has mapped a complete urban complex of office buildings, apartments, hotels and retail stores. They say a resident population of approximately 7,000 persons will be possible.

During the day hours over 60,000 is predicted. The amount of cars in this one small area becomes astronomical. Of course many levels of parking will be necessary and burying deep into the Hill will be a major undertaking.

Forgotten foundations might be stumbled upon. It is quite possible that the broken concrete supports of the old Major M. J. Wicks' mansion will be brought to the surface and for a brief moment the workmen might pause as though they heard the voice of this imposing gentleman calling to his chauffeur to ready the car for the opera that night.

37

The five-story Engstrum Hotel directly across from the Public Library on Fifth Street faces in the opposite direction from where the lofty mansions once stood. On all sides the pressure is mounting to allow progress to manifest itself in more office buildings that are tall, tailored, and highly terrestrial.

Or perhaps parts of the Louis Fry two-story duplex with its ornate Corinthian capitols and decorative railings will become entangled with the shoveled dirt. The solidly packed earth has a way of preserving the past in a very special way. No wind, rain, or sun can ever destroy or age whatever conceals itself beneath its layers.

And if the bulldozers should suddenly turn in a southerly direction towards what used to be South Grand Avenue, they would be right on the very boundary of the Myra Hershey estate. Right up to 1916 she kept her Norman-turreted stucco in mint condition for all her many friends and

guests. Whatever is left in the ground at this time, however, will hardly be recognized by even the former owner herself.

The future plans for Bunker Hill have almost a fantasy flavor about them: landscaped parks and plazas will greet visitors as they wander through the specially constructed pedestrian concourses.

The openness of this area will be considered a designer's concept of constructive space for each participating individual. Does that sound a little impersonal? Remember we are no longer dealing with individuals who take pride in the home in which they live but with blocks of impending population. Consider that there will be up to 12 million square feet of office space, one-half million square feet of retail space, and about 3,000 hotel rooms. Naturally the automobile must have its berth also. So far no invention has been patented which will fold up these metal conveyances so they can be quickly tucked into nearby convenient closets.

Jargon such as "downtown circulation distribution systems" sprinkled through the proposal attempt to minimize the congestion which will surely take place. With all the beautiful plans, the fact still remains that there is only so much room within 136 acres to live and breathe as God intended.

Originally this hilltop region had been esthetically divided by majestic mansions with surrounding grounds that allowed the flowers to bloom and the trees to expand. Man is no different: he is as much a part of nature as the unfolding plant. Give him undiluted space or he will die. Perhaps his death won't be a physical phenomenon but the dark reflection of his eyes will quickly reveal the soundless void within him.

Could the old mansions have been saved like the dwellings of the French Quarter in New Orleans or on Telegraph Hill in San Francisco? They say the old Angel's Flight had to be condemned because of the dangerous decay but how did this decay come about? Did the mechanism itself erode out of anger or was it merely ignored by those who were its guardians? Did those in power decide that the little cars were in the way of commercial progress? And was the ultimate dismissal of values the real cause of deterioration?

A promise was made in 1963 that the Angel's Flight would someday run again. This will no doubt be honored only with certain reservations. The new tract incline will be almost 50 percent less than the original and, according to an engineer's report, the length of the run will be about 50 feet shorter due to the increased setback at Olive and Hill Streets.

The original station and the Hill Street arch have been hit with dry rot; their structural soundness is questionable. Perhaps a clever artist will come upon the scene and be able to somehow restore portions of these treasured landmarks.

The bronze plaque and drinking fountain, placed at the original Angel's Flight by the Native Daughters of the Golden West, remains in good condition and will be used again.

What if this same attention had been given to the classic mansions of the past? Would a restored Bunker Hill have become an international tourist attraction and something even more? Generations of the future could see how patience and the realization of value molded a life with a lasting firmness of purpose. It is not a question of holding onto the past but rather respecting that which was once created for the good of all.

The original cable cars, Olivet and Sinai, will never be seen again climbing that certain section of the Hill. The original seats and iron work can possibly be incorporated into the new cars but the interior incline will never be the same.

The ease of movement and that turn-of-the-century inner contentment can never be recaptured in a highly industrialized society. Nevertheless, the awareness that Man best exists in open natural conditions shouldn't be forgotten. To have a special place where the tense city occupant can walk leisurely through the streets of the past among lovingly regenerated structures is a great psychological uplift. At that one moment he sees himself not as a punched computerized object but as the truly unfolding spirit that he is.

What would happen if by some quirk in time and space one of the old mansions did reappear at such an opportune moment as though it had dipped through a distant fog and decided for a brief time to be solid once more?

Perhaps it might be the old L. J. Rose house, which was once described as "the most beautiful example of the American Renaissance in Los Angeles." For a moment the viewer would be stunned by the rectangular tower windows and red brick chimney that edged a few feet higher than the metal spires at the end of each peaked roof.

A massive wall of granite surrounded the lot at various levels, enhancing the entrance way with a solidity and power rarely exhibited by private structures today. This wall wasn't meant to keep out trespassers but rather to frame the beauty of the three-story construction which was within its perimeter.

The broad front stairs of polished stone would guide the spellbound visitor directly onto a wide tiled veranda and then onto the entrance hall of antique oak with exquisitely paneled ceilings.

By this time the wanderer might be too enthralled to advance any further. Curiosity will win over in the end! The upstairs rooms had to be observed. Frescoed and medallion portraits of poets were positioned on the walls to look

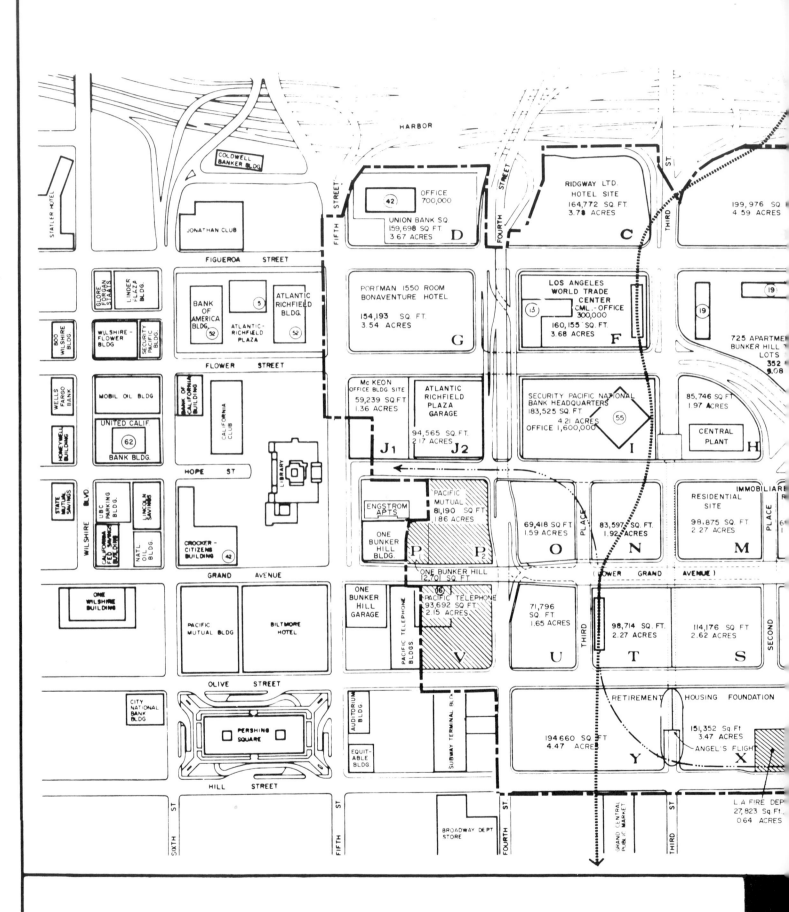

LAND DISPOSITION MAP

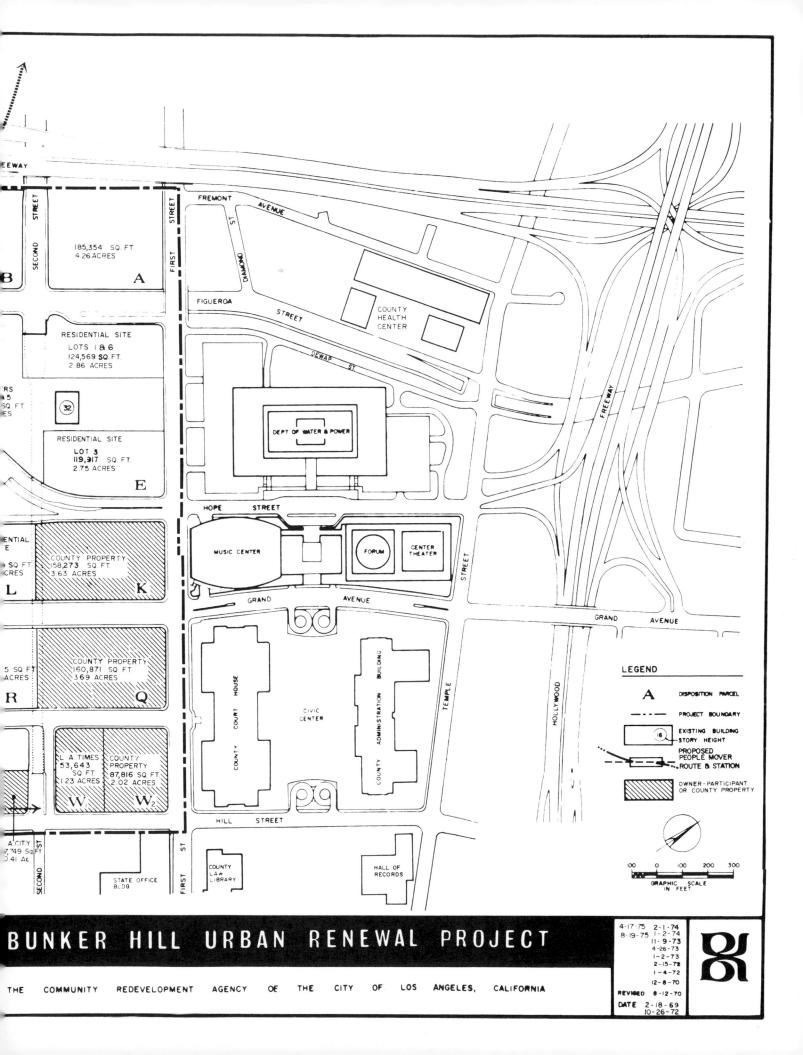

FREEWAY

SECOND STREET

185,354 SQ. FT.
4.26 ACRES

B   A

FIRST STREET

FREMONT

AVENUE

RESIDENTIAL SITE
LOTS 1 & 6
124,569 SQ. FT.
2.86 ACRES

FIGUEROA

DIAMOND ST

STREET

32

RESIDENTIAL SITE
LOT 3
119,917 SQ. FT.
2.75 ACRES

E

COUNTY
HEALTH
CENTER

DEWAP ST.

DEPT OF WATER & POWER

HOPE   STREET

RS
5
SQ FT
ES

ENTIAL
E
SQ FT
RES

COUNTY PROPERTY
158,273 SQ. FT.
3.63 ACRES

L   K

MUSIC CENTER

FORUM

CENTER
THEATER

STREET

FREEWAY

5 SQ FT
ACRES

COUNTY PROPERTY
160,871 SQ. FT.
3.69 ACRES

R   Q

GRAND   AVENUE

GRAND   AVENUE

HOLLYWOOD

L A TIMES
53,643
SQ. FT.
1.23 ACRES

COUNTY
PROPERTY
87,816 SQ. FT.
2.02 ACRES

W   W₂

COUNTY COURT HOUSE

CIVIC
CENTER

COUNTY ADMINISTRATION BUILDING

TEMPLE

LEGEND

A   DISPOSITION PARCEL

———   PROJECT BOUNDARY

16   EXISTING BUILDING
STORY HEIGHT

PROPOSED
PEOPLE MOVER
ROUTE & STATION

OWNER-PARTICIPANT
OR COUNTY PROPERTY

A CITY
7,749 SqFt
0.41 Ac

SECOND ST

HILL   STREET

FIRST ST

STATE OFFICE
BLDG

COUNTY
LAW
LIBRARY

HALL OF
RECORDS

100   0   100   200   300

GRAPHIC SCALE
IN FEET

BUNKER HILL URBAN RENEWAL PROJECT

THE   COMMUNITY   REDEVELOPMENT   AGENCY   OF   THE   CITY   OF   LOS   ANGELES,   CALIFORNIA

4-17-75   2-1-74
8-19-75   1-2-74
11-9-73
4-26-73
1-2-73
2-15-72
1-4-72
12-8-70
REVISED 8-12-70
DATE 2-18-69
10-26-72

g

The open boulevard heading south is modern-day Hill Street. On either side are the ubiquitous parking lots, and midway to the left is the former landing area of the old Angel's Flight.

down solemnly upon the readers of books in the spacious library.

All of these objects would quickly vanish the moment the viewer concentrated too hard on his own time and tensions. Of course the quiet grandeur of the golden days of Bunker Hill could not continue to exist. Nothing now remains of the past. If this were the year 1980 then the high-rise office buildings would flood his consciousness. Over $500 million will be spent for land acquisition and construction of buildings and this alone has the power to capture the mind of all those involved.

Much has been said about the justification of a city in taking private property for the so-called urban renewal process. Does government have a right to supersede "personal liberty" with plans of its own? Some hardened critics of this process say that the little people were forced out by the more powerful interests in a very legal manner.

The creation of the Community Redevelopment Agency made it possible for immediate clearance to begin. Some day that same indomitable process will take shape in reverse against the buildings yet to be constructed. Will they in turn be leveled and forgotten like the rest? If so, it is hard to imagine that there will be much sorrow with their passing.

Dwarfed by corporate
Newness,
The old Engstrum Hotel
Suspends its grilled marquee
From rusted
Links of the past.
Visible to all those
Who will
Look up
At its quiet majesty.

The great drama to bring water to Bunker Hill began in 1869 when the Los Angeles City Water Company began constructing reservoirs and pumping plants. Ten years earlier the principal method of delivering water to Los Angeles residents was by means of this large wooden water wheel that lifted water diverted from the Los Angeles River to a height sufficient to flow by gravity into the town.

In 1872 eleven miles of iron pipe were placed in the ground for the primary purpose of reaching the lofty mansions of Bunker Hill. Two reservoirs were constructed at an elevation of 240 feet to receive water from a steam-driven Hooker pump having a capacity of 40,000 gallons per hour.

Monthly charges for this service were divided into unique categories: bathing tubs in private homes, for each tub — 25 cents. For each private water closet — $1. Sprinkling gardens and grounds not more than 100 square yards in area — $1. Private horses, including water for washing carriages, for one horse — $1.

Picture taking in the late 1800s had its problems. It was often difficult to obtain detail. Faces and forms could easily become blurred. Here are members of the John Carl Zahn family at 427 S. Hope Street luxuriating on their open veranda in the cool afternoon of a summery 1891. Little if any definition is evident with the exception of the young boy standing by the stairway.

*Probably no home on top of the Hill in 1887 was more
alone than the one belonging to Mary Banning. Although
it seems to be quite isolated, the premises were actually
the scene of many parties and celebrations, and the dirt
road leading to the front entrance was well traveled.*

The churches surrounding the Bunker Hill area of the late 1800s were primarily fundamental. Rev. Benjamin Franklin Coulter believed in living near his wealthy congregation and had a lovely home on the Hill overlooking his high-steepled church down below.

One could take a leisurely ride down Third Street to the corner of Hill in the summer of 1898 without a thought of congestion. Residents on top of Bunker Hill had a direct route to the First Congregational Church on the right, and a number of stained glass windows were donated to the church by the wealthy members towering above in their three-story mansions.

47

A carriage ride up Second Street from Broadway to the top of Bunker Hill in 1887 was a slow, prodding process in comparison with today's heavy rush of traffic. Notice the two horses facing each other and sharing the same feed bag. Apparently their owners had no tight schedule to follow and weren't too worried that already half the day was gone.

All it took was a couple of sturdy mules and a sober driver to keep the passengers happy and moving in these early days of 1888. In the background is Judge Widney's palatial mansion on the top of Bunker Hill.

It would take some exceptional daring to balance one's self on this third-story, wrought-iron balcony outside the windows of the Edward Hildreth mansion at 357 S. Hope Street. Of course no resident of this very proper household would expose himself in such an undignified manner during the 1890s. Later when these private dwellings became rooming houses, it wasn't uncommon to see laundry flying in the wind or perhaps an adventurous sunbather lounging across the sun-blistered deck.

In this view looking up toward the top of Bunker Hill from Third Street, west of Spring, during the spring of 1888, the lofty mansions command the horizon. At night the lights from the open verandas could be seen for miles. The young boy in the sailor suit to the far right would be well over ninety today.

Not only has the residence of Rev. E. T. Hildreth completely vanished, but that former northwest corner of Hope Street has now become the southeast corner of the Security Pacific Plaza.

In 1895 Los Angeles had a population of 66,437 and was growing rapidly. It was a restless time in California history, one that was ideal for a young man going into the moving business. Martin Bekins specialized in handling household goods and could relocate a family up on top of Bunker Hill quickly and without the usual discomfort. Soon many affluent families were taking advantage of his services, and The Van & Storage Company was on its way to becoming an important link between the ordinary flatlands down below and the lofty mansions above.

No extra charge was made for the horse-drawn wagons that struggled up the side of Bunker Hill with their heavy loads. All goods had to be tied down to prevent a sudden unwelcome shift in weight. Young boys often beseeched the drivers for a ride to the top of the crest; the lucky ones got a chance to sit up front all the way.

The hotel business was not particularly good during the early years of the Bunker Hill development but this fact didn't keep builders from constructing a number of sprawling complexes to take care of a predicted influx of visitors. Businessmen were coming into Los Angeles in greater numbers and expected elegant accommodations. If the reputation of the hotels on top of Bunker Hill increased then the investors would surely reap a sizeable profit. All depended upon the economics of the country at the time. Fortunately they were on a definite upswing.

James Wesley Potts arrived in Los Angeles at the age of twenty-two and almost immediately saw the potential of an area soon to be called Bunker Hill. Since one of his many talents was making money, he could well afford to construct his own sprawling mansion and become a colorful part of the new social life of this fast growing city.

The dignified rococo styles of the Melrose Hotel (left) and the Richlieu (right) were meant to attract visiting businessmen to the Bunker Hill region. Thankfully, there was no such thing as television in these early times, or the nearby skyline would have been clogged with masses of aluminum tubing heading in all different directions.

The sprawling mansions (above) on top of Bunker Hill had plenty of space between them. The center mansion belonged to Fred Bauer. His enclosed balconies were the scene of many bright summer parties. Shown below is a view looking west from the Court House in 1898. To the left is the uncrowded Broadway Ave. and right is the Bradbury mansion.

About 1914 electric delivery trucks were active on top of Bunker Hill. Here is one of those grand old vehicles parked before a vine-covered cottage on Grand Avenue. Since there were no pneumatic tires in those days, the driver and his cargo had a rough ride over even the smoothest streets.

How many bricks do you count in these octagonally shaped chimneys on the side of the Crocker mansion at the corner of Olive and Third Street? The artisans who worked on this classic structure completed a new level each day, and the following morning they would stand at a distance to view their work from the day before. Pride and a real sense of accomplishment was in their labor. Today such workmanship is indeed difficult to find. In 1890 it was not that much of a rarity.

Looking up onto Bunker Hill in the year 1890, one can almost imagine the quiet pace of the community. There was no Angel's Flight or nearby noisy freeway to blur the thoughts. The idea that a smog report would be broadcast early in the morning was a touch of science fiction no one could ever have accepted.

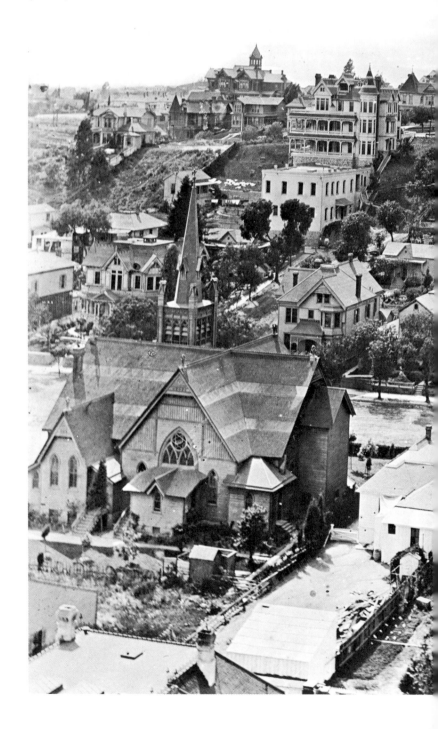

THE COURT FLIGHT

Residents of Bunker Hill during the year 1904 were pleased to hear the announcement that a new cable car would be constructed between First and Temple Streets, from Broadway to Court Street. That 200-foot elevation was a little too steep to handle at times.

To accommodate both the rider and walker, a stairway was also constructed beside the cable car. It took 47 steps to get to the first landing and an additional 93 to make it to the top.

For almost four decades the Court Flight ran on schedule with hardly any interruption. (A major overhaul took place in 1936, much to the dismay of the foot-weary residents on top of the Hill.)

Then when the surrounding land doubled in value, certain individuals saw the Flight as an obstruction to further growth in the Bunker Hill region. The land was needed for construction. More money and taxes would be available if there were buildings on that slanting site.

A mysterious fire swept over the wooden trestles during World War II (October 20, 1943). It was rumored that arson was involved. Nothing was ever proved, however, although newspaper reporters attempted to make a scandal of it.

Eventually, after further litigation against the property, a permit to abandon the facility was issued by the city during that same year. The faithful Court Flight was gone forever.

Looking down from Third Street on top of Bunker Hill in 1907, it was possible to view the lumbering streetcars coming from both directions. A trip to the beach was a long involved excursion.

Visiting businessmen staying at the Melrose Hotel often complained about the hanging vines at the Grand Street entrance. It was impossible to watch the passing traffic, which was part of the activity of the paying guest. The management explained that the vegetation deadened the sound of the passing cars, and they had no intention of ever cutting it down.

A Shriners convention in Los Angeles always meant that the hotels on top of Bunker Hill would be crowded by visiting delegates. Parking became a problem as can be seen from this congested street near Broadway and Fourth. The year is 1925, and the city is straining at the seams. The Hill was just beginning to become an "irritation" to those who saw the aloofness of its placid homes as a personal threat to progress.

The wide, tree-shaded walks of Pershing Square, only a few blocks away from the now-congested area of Bunker Hill, provided an ideal escape for the many lonely people who lived in tiny rooms and on limited pensions. The time is the mid-1950s, and in less than two decades even the folksy look of the park would also be gone.

In the late 1890s Pershing Square was known as the Sixth Street Park (the general had yet to become famous). Even in these early days, the winding paths and open benches were a pleasant meeting place for those who lived alone in the nearby rooming houses.

Checkers and chess were the main activity of the men who lived on Bunker Hill in those solitary rooming houses. It was only a short walk over to Pershing Square where a game was always in progress. You played to win, but more important was getting involved in one of the games and staying in there until the very end.

The open starkness of the present-day Pershing Square has
a futuristic blandness that is frightening. Gone is the lush
feel of a tropical California wonderland where the tired and
lonely folks from Bunker Hill and other nearby localities
could wander about and occasionally sit down to exchange
viewpoints. One no longer experiences the warmth of a
friendly park; even the nearby trees seem to be at rigid
attention, constantly guarded by the low concrete walls
around their trunks.

Like the extraction of a front tooth, the removal of the Angel's Flight from the side of Bunker Hill gives the land a sad look of desolation. The photo at left with the Flight in operation was taken in the late 1950s; the one above in the mid-1970s. A few signs have changed in the background and the tall hotels on the side are gone, but this seems almost unimportant in comparison with the loss of the little railroad.

Ben Abril was one of the small group of dedicated artists who preserved the memory of old Bunker Hill on canvas for later generations to see.

This towering gothic structure looming over the crest of Bunker Hill once had majestic overtones of grandeur. At the top left corner of the roof is the chiseled head of a wolf guarding this classic wooden edifice from any intruders. Actually, he is facing the wrong way because on the west side of the building is the commercial handiwork of modern-day advertisers. The contents of the billboard are unknown, but its newly constructed scaffolding attests to an active sales campaign by some enterprising southern California company.

Another view of the scale-model of Bunker Hill that was constructed during depression days by WPA draftsmen.

The old wooden stairway that leads to the second floor
of this once-classic home on Bunker Hill needed a number
of vertical and horizontal supports to keep the step from
sagging when this picture was taken in the 1950s. The
blooming flowers at the edge of the porch, however, show
that the occupants still had positive thoughts about the
future of the Hill, even though there had been no current
news to support it.

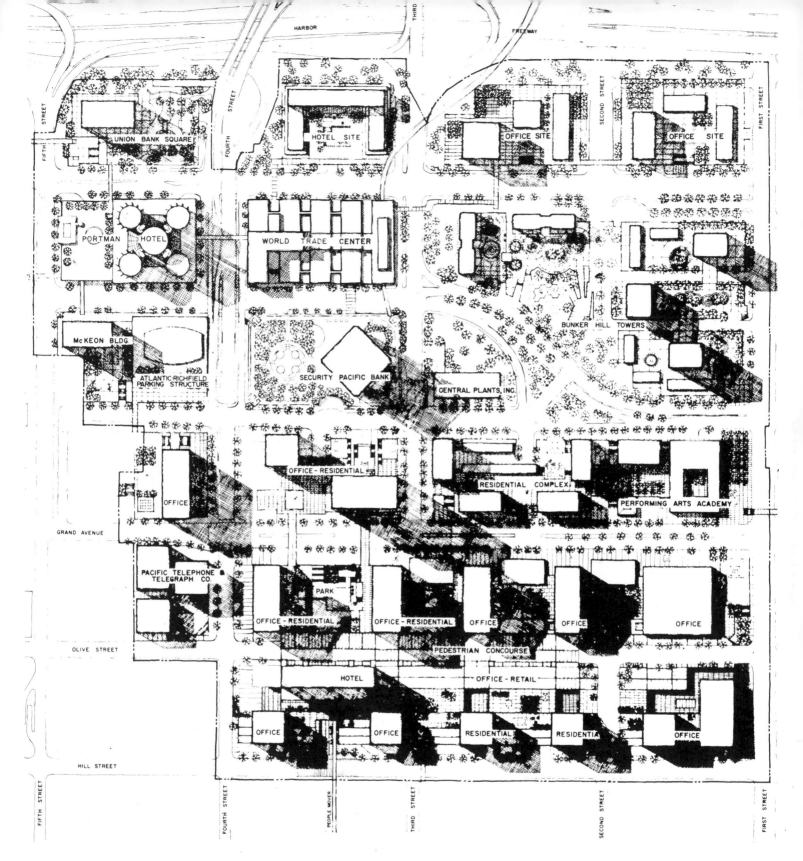

This illustrative plan by The Community Redevelopment Agency introduces the "new" Bunker Hill. Looking down at the buildings and parks, the proposed constructions seem marvelously symmetrical, but there is no longer a feeling of elevation. All is flat, blending prosaically into the hotels and office buildings on either side. Never again will there be that aesthetic separation between those who dream of the idyllic life and those who see only the materialistic view of survival.

71

LOS ANGELES, CAL

Here is a rare panoramic view of Los Angeles taken from an almost vacant region soon to be called Bunker Hill. The time is the summer of 1869, and few real estate dealers were interested in the property overlooking the city; it didn't seem

THURSDAY, MAY 13, 1869.

like a practical place to live. (1) New High Street. (2) Temple Block — South Wing. (3) Original U.S. Hotel. (4) Market Street. (5) Temple Market House. (6) Court Street. (7) House of ex-Mayor, J. G. Nichols.

BUNKER HILL
ARCHITECTURE

longer were heavy timbers necessary for the construction of a house. Cheap Douglas fir was plentiful, and it was possible to purchase a cottage for $2,000, or a spacious two-story house for about $5,000.

The concept of the frame house allowed all sorts of bizarre invention. The basic arrangement consisted of two stories rising from a square floor plan. Porches and "extra rooms" were joined to the main cube. The final architectural delineation completely depended on the whims of the owner. Perhaps he would enjoy a solarium directly facing the rising sun. Then again, an octagonal library overlooking the city might provide an interesting conversation piece.

Walking along these newly populated streets, a visitor could not help being amazed at the divergent styles seen on either side. High-pitched roofs trimmed in ornamental molding gave certain plain structures a pontifical look. Others, heavily trimmed with spangled bracelets beneath jutting eaves, featured a roof that swooped up to a token "widow's walk" in the center.

One very popular design favored by those of ostentatious taste was the "rope pattern," which could easily be blended into various trimmings with elegant results.

Steam-powered saws in Los Angeles lumberyards worked long hours to supply busy builders on top of the Hill. Once the timber was prepared, there was still the difficult job of delivery. The narrow thoroughfares didn't make it easy. More than once, someone's well-trimmed backyard was used as a necessary shortcut to the construction site.

The following photographs show random examples of the styles of architecture prevalent on Bunker Hill. Although taken in later years, they nonetheless illustrate the glories of a bygone time.

It was reported in the Los Angeles Daily News on March 3, 1872, that "the surrounding hills overlooking the city were beginning to lose their freshness of color." One reason for this change was the sudden upsurge in building taking place in an area soon to be known as Bunker Hill. Anyone arriving in the city of Los Angeles who was even rumored to be a carpenter, mason, or bricklayer was offered immediate work.

Everyone had his own idea what a mansion on top of the Hill should look like. Adobe architecture was dismissed by the wealthy residents as being much too bourgeois. Quasi-Greek temples and Neopolitan edifices were considered more desirable, even though they might shock the farmers and other common folk down below.

And so it was that structures featuring sprawling piazzas, ornate balconies, circling verandas, and elongated bay windows began to take form on the various narrow streets of the Hill. A new building technique known as the "balloon frame," which used nailed 2 x 4's in combination, was introduced during the Bunker Hill boom. No

The picturesque Victorian buildings which once distinguished Bunker Hill were being replaced in the 1970s by high-rise structures such as the Bonaventure Hotel, pictured here.